by Iain Gray

79 Main Street, Newtongrange,
Midlothian EH22 4NA
Tel: 0131 344 0414 Fax: 0845 075 6085
E-mail: info@lang-syne.co.uk
www.langsyneshop.co.uk

Design by Dorothy Meikle
Printed by Ricoh Print Scotland

ISBN 978-1-85217-542-9

Powell

MOTTO:
Looking up.

CREST:
A green griffin emerging from a crown.

NAME variations include:
Powel

Chapter one:

The origins of popular surnames

by George Forbes and Iain Gray

If you don't know where you came from, you won't know where you're going **is a frequently quoted observation and one that has a particular resonance today when there has been a marked upsurge in interest in genealogy, with increasing numbers of people curious to trace their family roots.**

Main sources for genealogical research include census returns and official records of births, marriages and deaths – and the key to unlocking the detail they contain is obviously a family surname, one that has been 'inherited' and passed from generation to generation.

No matter our station in life, we all have a surname – but it was not until about the middle of the fourteenth century that the practice of being identified by a particular surname became commonly established throughout the British Isles.

Previous to this, it was normal for a person to be identified through the use of only a forename.

But as population gradually increased and there were many more people with the same forename, surnames were adopted to distinguish one person, or community, from another.

Many common English surnames are patronymic in origin, meaning they stem from the forename of one's father – with 'Johnson,' for example, indicating 'son of John.'

It was the Normans, in the wake of their eleventh century conquest of Anglo-Saxon England, a pivotal moment in the nation's history, who first brought surnames into usage – although it was a gradual process.

For the Normans, these were names initially based on the title of their estates, local villages and chateaux in France to distinguish and identify these landholdings.

Such grand descriptions also helped enhance the prestige of these warlords and generally glorify their lofty positions high above the humble serfs slaving away below in the pecking order who had only single names, often with Biblical connotations as in Pierre and Jacques.

The only descriptive distinctions among the peasantry concerned their occupations, like 'Pierre the swineherd' or 'Jacques the ferryman.'

Roots of surnames that came into usage in England not only included Norman-French, but also Old French, Old Norse, Old English, Middle English, German, Latin, Greek, Hebrew and the Gaelic languages of the Celts.

The Normans themselves were originally Vikings, or 'Northmen', who raided, colonised and eventually settled down around the French coastline.

The had sailed up the Seine in their longboats in 900AD under their ferocious leader Rollo and ruled the roost in north eastern France before sailing over to conquer England in 1066 under Duke William of Normandy – better known to posterity as William the Conqueror, or King William I of England.

Granted lands in the newly-conquered England, some of their descendants later acquired territories in Wales, Scotland and Ireland – taking not only their own surnames, but also the practice of adopting a surname, with them.

But it was in England where Norman rule and custom first impacted, particularly in relation to the adoption of surnames.

This is reflected in the famous *Domesday Book*, a massive survey of much of England and Wales, ordered by William I, to determine who owned what, what it was worth and therefore how much they were liable to pay in taxes to the voracious Royal Exchequer.

Completed in 1086 and now held in the National Archives in Kew, London, 'Domesday' was an Old English word meaning 'Day of Judgement.'

This was because, in the words of one contemporary chronicler, "its decisions, like those of the Last Judgement, are unalterable."

It had been a requirement of all those English landholders – from the richest to the poorest – that they identify themselves for the purposes of the survey and for future reference by means of a surname.

This is why the *Domesday Book*, although written in Latin as was the practice for several centuries with both civic and ecclesiastical records, is an invaluable source for the early appearance of a wide range of English surnames.

Several of these names were coined in connection with occupations.

These include Baker and Smith, while Cooks, Chamberlains, Constables and Porters were to be found carrying out duties in large medieval households.

The church's influence can be found in names such as Bishop, Friar and Monk while the popular name of Bennett derives from the late fifth to mid-sixth century Saint Benedict, founder of the Benedictine order of monks.

The early medical profession is represented by Barber, while businessmen produced names that include Merchant and Sellers.

Down at the village watermill, the names that cropped up included Millar/Miller, Walker and Fuller, while other self-explanatory trades included Cooper, Tailor, Mason and Wright.

Even the scenery was utilised as in Moor, Hill, Wood and Forrest – while the hunt and the chase supplied names that include Hunter, Falconer, Fowler and Fox.

Colours are also a source of popular surnames, as in Black, Brown, Gray/Grey, Green and White, and would have denoted the colour of the clothing the person habitually wore or, apart from the obvious exception of 'Green', one's hair colouring or even complexion.

The surname Red developed into Reid, while

Blue was rare and no-one wanted to be associated with yellow.

Rather self-important individuals took surnames that include Goodman and Wiseman, while physical attributes crept into surnames such as Small and Little.

Many families proudly boast the heraldic device known as a Coat of Arms, as featured on our front cover.

The central motif of the Coat of Arms would originally have been what was borne on the shield of a warrior to distinguish himself from others on the battlefield.

Not featured on the Coat of Arms, but highlighted on page three, is the family motto and related crest – with the latter frequently different from the central motif.

Adding further variety to the rich cultural heritage that is represented by surnames is the appearance in recent times in lists of the 100 most common names found in England of ones that include Khan, Patel and Singh – names that have proud roots in the vast sub-continent of India.

Echoes of a far distant past can still be found in our surnames and they can be borne with pride in commemoration of our forebears.

Chapter two:

Repelling the invaders

A name of ancient roots, Powell is ranked 87th in some lists of the 100 most common surnames found in England but, in common with several other names that feature in these lists, it is particularly identified with Wales.

It derives from the personal name 'Howel', or 'Howell' – also sometimes rendered as 'Hoel' – which, in turn, derives from the Old Welsh 'Hywel' or 'Houel.'

The Old Welsh forms of the given name are said to indicate either 'son of the servant of St Paul' or 'eminent' while, as a surname, 'Powell' incorporates the Welsh prefix 'ap', meaning 'son of.'

This means that the original 'ap-Hoel', for example, through the course of time became 'Powell.'

Adding further richness and colour to the origin of the name is that it also boasts Celtic roots.

This is through the Old Celtic 'pa', meaning 'son of' and rendered, for example, as 'Pa Howell', rendered in later centuries as 'Powell.'

Undoubtedly, flowing through the veins

today of many bearers of the Powell name is the blood of the ancient Britons.

Of Celtic pedigree, these early inhabitants of the British Isles were settled for centuries from a line south of the River Forth in Scotland all the way down to the south coast of England and with a particular presence in Wales.

Speaking a Celtic language known as Brythonic, they boasted a glorious culture that flourished even after the Roman invasion of Britain in 43 AD and the subsequent consolidation of Roman power by about 84 AD.

With many of the original Britons absorbing aspects of Roman culture, they became 'Romano-British' – while still retaining their own proud Celtic heritage.

Following the withdrawal of the last Roman legions from Britain in 406, what is now modern-day Wales, or *Cymru*, fragmented into a number of independent kingdoms – with the most powerful king being recognised as overall ruler.

Recognised as King of the Britons, he had to battle with not only internal rivals but also the depredations of the wild sea rovers known as the Vikings, or Northmen.

There were also the Anglo-Saxons to contend with – as those Germanic tribes who invaded and settled in the south and east of the island of Britain from about the early fifth century were known.

These Anglo-Saxons were composed of the Jutes, from the area of the Jutland Peninsula in modern Denmark, the Saxons from Lower Saxony, in modern Germany and the Angles from the Angeln area of Germany.

It was the Angles who gave the name 'Engla land', or 'Aengla land' – better known as 'England.'

The Anglo-Saxons held sway in what became known as England from approximately 550 to 1066, with the main kingdoms those of Sussex, Wessex, Northumbria, Mercia, Kent, East Anglia and Essex.

Whoever controlled the most powerful of these kingdoms was tacitly recognised as overall 'king' – one of the most noted being Alfred the Great, King of Wessex from 871 to 899.

The Anglo-Saxons, meanwhile, had usurped the power of the indigenous Britons, such as those found in Wales, and who referred to them as 'Saeson' or 'Saxones.'

It is from this that the Scottish Gaelic term

for 'English people' of 'Sasannach' derives, the Irish Gaelic 'Sasanach' and the Welsh 'Saeson.'

The first serious shock to Anglo-Saxon control of England came in 789 in the form of sinister black-sailed Viking ships that appeared over the horizon off the island monastery of Lindisfarne, in the northeast of the country.

The island was sacked in an orgy of violence and plunder, setting the scene for what would be many more terrifying raids on the coastlines of not only England, but also Wales, Ireland and Scotland.

One famous ancestor of some who would later adopt the Powell name, from the forename 'Hywel', was the ninth century Rhodri the Great, known in Welsh as Rhodri Mawr or Rhodri ap Merfyn.

This descent is through his grandson, the Welsh king Hywel Dda "the Good" ap Cadell, who ruled from about 880 to 950.

His famed grandfather, Rhodri, born in about 820, was the first to rule most of what would become present-day Wales.

Inheriting the kingdom of Gwynedd on the death of his father in 844, he went on to gain the other powerful kingdoms of Powys and Seisyllwg – but he faced twin threats from the Vikings and the Anglo-Saxons.

Victorious in battle over the Vikings in 865, killing their leader Gorm, he had to flee for a time to Ireland after giving battle to them twenty years later on Anglesey.

Back in his native Wales a year later, both he and his son Gwriad were killed in battle in 878 against the Anglo-Saxon Ceolwulf II of Mercia.

The death knell of Anglo-Saxon supremacy and also what remained of Welsh independence was sounded with the Norman Conquest of 1066.

By this date, England had become a nation with several powerful competitors to the throne.

In what were extremely complex family, political and military machinations, the monarch was Harold II, who had succeeded to the throne following the death of Edward the Confessor.

But his right to the throne was contested by two powerful competitors – his brother-in-law King Harold Hardrada of Norway, in alliance with Tostig, Harold II's brother, and Duke William II of Normandy.

In what has become known as The Year of Three Battles, Hardrada invaded England and gained victory over the English king on September 20 at the battle of Fulford, in Yorkshire.

Five days later, however, Harold II decisively defeated his brother-in-law and brother at the battle of Stamford Bridge.

But he had little time to celebrate his victory, having to immediately march south from Yorkshire to encounter a mighty invasion force led by Duke William of Normandy that had landed at Hastings, in East Sussex.

Harold's battle-hardened but exhausted force of Anglo-Saxon soldiers confronted the Normans on October 14, with Harold drawing up a strong defensive position at the top of Senlac Hill, building a shield wall to repel Duke William's cavalry and infantry.

The Normans suffered heavy losses, but through a combination of the deadly skill of their archers and the ferocious determination of their cavalry they eventually won the day.

Anglo-Saxon morale had collapsed on the battlefield as word spread through the ranks that Harold had been killed.

William was declared King of England on December 25, and the complete subjugation of his Anglo-Saxon subjects followed.

Those Normans who had fought on his behalf were rewarded with the lands of Anglo-Saxons, many of whom sought exile abroad as mercenaries.

Within an astonishingly short space of time, Norman manners, customs and law were imposed on England – laying the basis for what subsequently became established 'English' custom and practice.

In 1282, by which time most of Wales had come under Anglo-Norman rule, final rebellion against this was crushed by England's Edward I, and it is from this date that the heir apparent to the British throne has borne the title of Prince of Wales.

An abortive rebellion was led in the early fifteenth century by the freedom fighter Owain Glyndŵr, while in the following century, under Henry VIII, Wales was 'incorporated' into the English kingdom; in 1707, in common with Scotland, Wales became part of the United Kingdom.

Chapter three:

Lives of adventure

Bearers of the proud name of Powell have stamped a distinctive mark on the historical record through a diverse range of endeavours and pursuits.

Born in 1796, Baden Powell was the English mathematician and Church of England clergyman who, in addition to holding the Savilian Chair of Geometry at Oxford University from 1827 to 1860, held views on evolution that preceded those more famously proposed later by Charles Darwin.

A Fellow of the Royal Geographical Society, it was after his death in 1860 that, in his memory, his family changed their surname to 'Baden-Powell.'

Married three times, he was the father of fourteen children – one of the most renowned being Robert Baden-Powell, 1st Baron Baden-Powell, founder of what is now the worldwide Scouting Movement.

Born in 1857 in Paddington, London, he served with great distinction in the British Army in India and Africa – while during the Second Boer War of 1899 to 1902, he successfully defended the town of Mafeking, South Africa.

As garrison commander, in what became known as the Siege of Mafeking, he held off a force of more than 8,000 Boers over a period of 217 days before the town was relieved.

Much of his success was largely attributable to deception tactics he employed, including the planting of fake minefields, while he personally undertook reconnaissance, or scouting, missions into the enemy lines.

Many of the techniques he used on these scouting missions found their way into military manuals.

His *Aids to Scouting* was adapted in 1908 for a youth readership as his famous *Scouting for Boys* – which holds the record as the fourth best-selling book of the twentieth century.

Only a few months before the first publication, he had held a camp for about twenty boys on Brownsea Island, Dorset, and from this early beginning was laid the foundation for what became the Boy Scouts, or Scouting Movement.

Running parallel to this movement was the Girl Guide Movement, formalised in 1910 under the leadership of his sister Agnes Baden-Powell.

Elevated to the Peerage of the United

Kingdom in 1929 as Baron Baden-Powell, of Gilwell, in the County of Essex, Gilwell Park later became the International Scout Leader training centre; he died in 1941.

Another adventurous bearer of the Powell name was the American geologist and explorer John Wesley Powell.

Born in 1834 in Mount Morris, New York, the son of a preacher who had emigrated four years earlier from Shrewsbury, England, he studied at a number of colleges after the family moved westward to Ohio and then Wisconsin.

Fascinated by the great outdoors and the natural sciences, as a young man he embarked on a number of trips through the Mississippi River Valley, while in 1856 he rowed the river from St Anthony, Minnesota, to the sea.

He is best known, however, for the 1869 Powell Geographical Expedition that involved a three-month trip down the Green and Colorado rivers and also included the first passage through the Grand Canyon.

Director of the U.S. Geological Survey from 1881 to 1894 and director of the Bureau of Ethnology at the Smithsonian Institution, he died in 1902; Lake

Powell, a reservoir on the Colorado River, is named in his honour.

Another well-travelled bearer of the Powell name was the American journalist, war correspondent and author Edward Alexander Powell, born in 1879 in Syracuse, New York and better known as E. Alexander Powell.

Beginning his career as a journalist with the *Syracuse Journal* and later working for a time in London for a typewriter manufacturer, he was based in the Near East as a special correspondent for a number of American and British publications from 1905 to 1906.

The years 1906 to 1909 saw the globe-trotting Powell as a U.S. Consular Official in Syria and Egypt.

Serving for a time during the First World War as a war correspondent and later as a captain in U.S. military intelligence, much of his war journalism was published in a range of magazines and newspapers that included the *New York World* and the British *Daily Mail*.

Turning his talents to adventure and travel writing, before his death in 1957 he was the author of a wide range of popular books that include his 1925 *Beyond the Utmost Purple Rim*.

In what is the often cut-throat world of politics, John Enoch Powell, better known as Enoch Powell, was not only a British politician but also a soldier, eminent classical scholar, poet, linguist and author.

Born in 1912, he was reading Ancient Greek by the time he was aged only five and he would go on to learn a total of twelve languages throughout his lifetime – including Hebrew, eight years before his death.

Reaching the rank of brigadier serving in both intelligence and staff positions during the Second World War, what was to prove a stormy career in politics began in 1950 when he was elected a Conservative Member of Parliament (MP), going on to serve in a number of posts that included, from 1960 to 1963, Minister of Health.

His downfall in the Conservative Party came in 1968 when he was dismissed from his Shadow Cabinet post of Defence Secretary after making a highly controversial speech on race and immigration – referred to as the "Rivers of Blood" speech – in which he warned of what he perceived as the dangers of violent racial discord breaking out in Britain.

Leaving the Conservative Party in 1974, he

joined the Ulster Unionist Party (UUP), serving as one of its MPs in the Commons from 1974 until eleven years before his death in 1998.

Born in 1941, Charles Powell is the British diplomat, politician and businessman who, after joining the Diplomatic Service in 1963, went on to serve from 1983 to 1990 as Private Secretary to Conservative Prime Minister Margaret Thatcher and then in the same role from 1990 to 1991 to her successor, John Major.

Created a life peer in 2000 as Baron Powell of Bayswater, he is the brother of Jonathan Powell, born in 1956, who served as Chief of Staff to Tony Blair throughout his tenure from 1997 to 2007 as Labour Prime Minister.

Across the Atlantic, Colin Powell is the Unites States retired four-star general and statesman born in 1937 in Manhattan to Jamaican immigrant parents.

During his 35 years as a professional soldier he held a number of high level positions that included, from 1987 to 1989, that of National Security Advisor, Commander of the U.S. Army Forces Command and, during America's first war with Iraq known as Operation Desert Storm, Chairman of the

Joint Chiefs of Staff – a post he held from 1989 to 1993.

In the political sphere, he served from 2001 to 2005 as Secretary of State under President George W. Bush – the first African-American to hold the post.

A number of schools and other institutions across the United States have been named in his honour, while he is also the recipient of many awards that include the Congressional Gold Medal, two Presidential Medals of Freedom, the President's Citizens Medal and the Ronald Regan Freedom Award.

Chapter four:

On the world stage

Born in 1944 in Salford, Lancashire, Robert Powell is the English film and television actor best known for his roles of Jesus in the acclaimed 1977 two-part television film *Jesus of Nazareth* and of Richard Hannay in the 1978 *The Thirty Nine Steps*.

His role in *Jesus of Nazareth*, directed by Franco Zeffirelli and whose other stars included Laurence Olivier, Rod Steiger, James Mason and Christopher Plummer, won him a BAFTA nomination and the *TV Times* Best Actor Award.

Other film roles include the 1969 *The Italian Job* and the 1986 *Shaka Zulu*, while television credits include *The Detectives* and the popular BBC medical drama *Holby City*.

Across the Atlantic from British shores, **William Powell** was the American actor best known for having starred in a number of films with Myrna Lloyd, including *The Thin Man* series based on books by the novelist Dashiell Hammett.

His many credits include the 1934 *The Thin*

Man, the 1936 *My Man Godfrey* and, starring beside Clark Gable, the 1934 *Manhattan Melodrama*.

Born in 1892 in Pittsburgh, Pennsylvania and the recipient of a star on the Hollywood Walk of Fame, he died in 1984.

Also the recipient of a star on the Hollywood Walk of Fame, **Dick Powell** was the American singer, actor and film producer whose film credits include *Gold Diggers of 1933*, *Gold Diggers of 1935*, the 1941 *In the Navy* and, from 1958, *The Hunters*.

Born in 1904 in Mountain View, Arkansas, he died in 1963.

Behind the camera lens, **Michael Powell**, born in 1905 in Bekesbourne, Kent, the son of a hop farmer, was the noted English film director best known for his work with fellow director Emeric Pressburger.

It was along with Pressburger and working together under the name The Archers, that he was responsible for a number of British film classics.

These are *49th Parallel*, from 1941, the 1943 *The Life and Death of Colonel Blimp*, the 1946 *A Matter of Life and Death*, the 1947 *Black Narcissus*, the 1948 *The Red Shoes* and, from 1951, *The Tales of Hoffmann*; he died in 1990.

Born in London in 1963, **John Powell** is the English composer and conductor known for his scores for a number of films.

A graduate of Trinity College of Music, London, his score for the 2010 *How to Train Your Dragon* won an Academy Award nomination.

Other films for which he has written the scores include the 1997 *Face/Off*, the 2003 *The Bourne Supremacy*, the 2006 *The Bourne Ultimatum* and, from 2008, *Kung Fu Panda*.

Also behind the camera lens, **Sandy Powell** is the British costume designer born in London in 1960.

The recipient of three Academy Awards – for the 1999 *Shakespeare in Love*, the 2005 *The Aviator* and the 2010 *The Young Victoria* – she is also the recipient of a BAFTA Award for the latter film and for the 1999 *Velvet Goldmine*.

She is also the recipient of an OBE in recognition of her work.

Born in 1901 in Bridgworth, Shropshire, **Dilys Powell** was the distinguished British literary and film critic who worked for many years with *The Sunday Times* newspaper.

Also one of the founding members in the early 1950s of the Independent Television Authority

(ITA), before her death in 1995 she was also the author of a number of books that include her 1973 *The Villa Ariadne* and the 1991 *The Dilys Powell Film Reader*.

On radio, Peter James Barnard-Powell is the English former disc jockey better known as **Peter Powell**.

Born in Birmingham in 1951, he was a popular disc jockey in the late 1970s and in the 1980s on BBC Radio One; now pursuing a career in talent management, he was married from 1990 to 1998 to television presenter Anthea Turner.

Bearers of the Powell name have also excelled in the highly competitive world of sport.

Born in 1963 in Philadelphia, **Mike Powell** is the American former track and field athlete who, at the time of writing, still holds the world record for the long jump.

This was set at the 1991 World Championships in Tokyo, when he jumped 8.95 metres, 5cm. longer than the previous record.

The feat won him the James E. Sullivan Award and BBC Sports Personality of the Year, Overseas Personality Award in 1991, while he also won silver medals at the 1988 and 1992 Olympics.

Born in 1982 in Spanish Town, Jamaica, **Asafa Powell** is the sprinter who, between June of 2005 and May of 2008, held the world record for the 100-metres event.

These were for times of 9.77 and 9.74 seconds respectively, while he also won a gold medal as a member of the Jamaican 4x100-metres relay team at the 2008 Olympics and gold in the 100-metres at the 2006 Commonwealth Games.

On the fields of European football, **Hope Powell** is the English former international women's footballer who won 33 caps playing for her nation from 1983, when she was aged only 16, until 1998.

Manager of the England Women Team from 1998 and the Great Britain and Northern Ireland Women's Olympic team from 2012, the former mid-fielder scored 35 goals while playing for England.

Born in 1966 in Lewisham, she is the recipient of both an OBE and a CBE and an inductee of the English Football Hall of Fame.

Also on the football pitch, **Ivor Powell**, born in 1916 in Bargoed, Wales, won eight caps playing for his nation between 1946 and 1950.

Recognised as one of the finest players of his generation, he played as a wing half for clubs that include Queens Park Rangers, Aston Villa and Bradford City, while he later managed teams that include Port Vale, Bradford City and Carlisle United; he died in 2012.

On the rugby pitch, **Andy Powell**, born in Brecon in 1981, has played for both the Wales national rugby union team and the British and Irish Lions.

In a much different sporting discipline, **Caroline Powell** is the equestrian born in 1973 in Lower Hutt, New Zealand.

Winning the bronze medal in Team eventing at the 2002 Olympics, she was also the winner in 2010 of the Burghley Horse Trials.

Born in 1916 in Greenville, Alabama, **William J. Powell** was the American entrepreneur and golf course owner who designed and opened America's first racially integrated club – the Clearview Golf Club, in East Canton, Ohio.

Famous for his remark: "The only colour that matters is the colour of the greens" and a recipient of the Professional Golfers Association (PGA) Distinguished Service Award, he died in 2009.

From sport to the world of literature, **Anthony Dymoke Powell** was the English novelist renowned for *A Dance to the Music of Time* – a twelve-volume work published between 1951 and 1975.

Including the first in the work, *A Question of Upbringing* and the final *Hearing Secret Harmonies*, *A Dance to the Music of Time* has remained in continuous print and been adapted for a number of radio and television productions.

Born in 1905 in Westminster, he was named by *The Times* newspaper eight years after his death in 2000 in its list of "The 50 Greatest British Writers Since 1945."

From literature to rock music, Colin Flooks, born in 1947 in Cirencester, Gloucestershire and better known as **Cozy Powell**, was the legendary English drummer who, after taking up the drumsticks when aged 12, went on to play for bands that included The Jeff Beck Group, Rainbow, Whitesnake and Black Sabbath; he died in 1998.

Also behind the drums, **Don Powell**, born in 1946 in Bilston, Wolverhampton is the musician and songwriter better known as one of the original members of the British glam rock band Slade.

Born in 1950 in Stepney, London, **Andy Powell** is the rock guitarist and songwriter best known as a founding member in 1969 of the band Wishbone Ash.

From rock to jazz, Earl Rudolph Powell, better known as **Buddy Powell**, was the American pianist recognised as having played an important role in the development of the genre known as bebop.

Born in 1924 in Harlem, New York, and having played with other musicians who included Sonny Rollins, Miles Davis and Art Blakey, he died in 1966.

An American jazz pianist and composer of classical music, **Mel Powell** was the winner of the Pulitzer Prize for Music in 1990.

Born Melvin Epstein in 1923 in the Bronx, New York City and having played for a time during the Second World War with Glenn Miller's Army Air Force Band, he won the Pulitzer Prize for his *Duplicates: A Concerto for Two Pianos and Orchestra*; he died in 1998.

Remembered for having composed the music for the famous First World War marching song *Pack Up Your Troubles in Your Old Kit Bag*, **Felix Powell** was the British Army staff sergeant born in 1878 in St Asaph, Wales.

Under the pseudonym George Asaf, the

words were written by his younger brother **George Powell**, born in 1880.

Written in 1915 in response to a competition for "best morale-building song", it won first prize and has subsequently been described as "perhaps the most optimistic song ever written."

Serving throughout the First World War, Felix Powell tragically took his own life in 1942 while serving in the Home Guard.

Rather ironically, while the brothers had made a significant contribution to British wartime morale through their song, George Powell was a pacifist and became a conscientious objector when military conscription was imposed a year after the song was written; he died in 1951.